Leaders

in a week

CAROL A. O'CONNOR Ph.D.

Hodder & Stoughton

A MEMBER OF THE HODDER HEADLINE GROUP

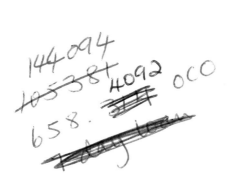

Orders: please contact Bookpoint Ltd, 130 Milton Park, Abingdon, Oxon OX14
4SB. Telephone: (44) 01235 827720, Fax: (44) 01235 400454. Lines are open from
9.00 - 6.00, Monday to Saturday, with a 24 hour message answering service.
Email address: orders@bookpoint.co.uk

British Library Cataloguing in Publication Data
A catalogue record for this title is available from The British Library

ISBN 0 340 84951 7

First published 1994
Impression number   10 9 8 7 6 5 4 3 2 1
Year   2007 2006 2005 2004 2003 2002

Typeset by SX Composing DTP, Rayleigh, Essex.
Printed in Great Britain for Hodder & Stoughton Educational, a division of
Hodder Headline Plc, 338 Euston Road, London NW1 3BH by Cox & Wyman,
Reading, Berkshire.

chartered
management
institute

inspiring leaders

The leading organisation for professional management

As the champion of management, the Chartered Management Institute shapes and supports the managers of tomorrow. By sharing intelligent insights and setting standards in management development, the Institute helps to deliver results in a dynamic world.

Setting and raising standards

The Institute is a nationally accredited organisation, responsible for setting standards in management and recognising excellence through the award of professional qualifications.

Encouraging development, improving performance

The Institute has a vast range of development programmes, qualifications, information resources and career guidance to help managers and their organisations meet new challenges in a fast-changing environment.

Shaping opinion

With in-depth research and regular policy surveys of its 91,000 individual members and 520 corporate members, the Chartered Management Institute has a deep understanding of the key issues. Its view is informed, intelligent and respected.

For more information call 01536 204222 or visit www.managers.org.uk

C O N T E N T S

Opportunities for leadership occur every day, so that even the most reluctant individuals occasionally find themselves in charge. The better prepared they are to meet these leadership challenges, the more readily they develop new skills and increase their confidence and personal insight.

Leadership skill can be acquired through training and effort even if background, modesty, lack of confidence or inexperience create self-doubt. This process often begins when individuals discover that they have qualities and strengths usually associated with leadership. They then surprise themselves with their own inner resources. When this kind of inner strength is revealed, its existence is not easily forgotten. Regular exercise of new-found strength produces further achievement and a sense of self-fulfilment so that growth leads to growth.

Each situation is different. Although important occasions are glamorous and attention-getting, more routine events benefit leadership development as well. Each and every chance to lead provides valuable practice and experience. This is preparation for major events in the future.

Potential leaders also need to recognise that along with the role comes responsibility. Taking charge is never easy and effective leadership requires considerable effort. This means pressure, stress and challenge, but also immense satisfaction when a task is successfully achieved.

Because most people are followers much of the time, part of every effort to develop leadership should include skills of following as well. The two sets of skills are complementary.

A skilled supporter knows how to contribute to a leader's success, while a good leader serves the needs of supporters to their mutual benefit.

Seven areas are essential for successful leadership. Using a step-by-step approach, these basics can be explored during the course of a week. The purpose is to improve leadership performance in both major and minor roles by recognising what needs to change and practising the necessary skills.

Steps to successful leadership
- Developing awareness
- Understanding people
- Power and authority
- Communication
- Decision-making
- Creating a vision
- Taking charge

Developing awareness

The first step to successful leadership is development of self-awareness. Leaders need to take time to reflect on the strengths and weaknesses of their own behaviour. This provides a basis for improving performance as well as increasing confidence and understanding other people. Leaders who lack personal insight are like tone-deaf musicians. Even if they acquire technical accuracy through drill and practice, they begin each performance at a distinct disadvantage. They need a sense of art as well as science in order to recognise when they have hit a sour note.

Today's programme covers four aspects for the development of self-awareness. These are:

- Leadership basics
- Self-assessment
- Following the leader
- Personal development

Leadership basics

There are three commonly accepted beliefs about leadership:

- leaders are born to their role
- certain qualities make a leader, such as ambition, charisma, confidence, initiative, independence, creativity, a sense of responsibility, among many others
- situations create leaders who adapt their behaviour to meet the needs of a specific group, time or place

All three of these ideas appear in various forms throughout history, and their serious study has dominated military and business science in this century. Although the debate about the nature of leadership continues, each approach has its firm advocates. Even so, one issue is consistently relevant regardless of personal beliefs. This is that leadership success depends upon the development of a positive relationship between leaders and supporters. The best leaders value their supporters and demonstrate this through their actions.

They know that respect is earned. It is the leaders' attitude towards their followers which inspires loyalty. This is far more important than birthright, personal qualities, a specific situation or a combination of all of these. Supporters are important because without them, leadership exists only in the imagination of the would-be leader. Without endorsement from these supporters, leaders lack power to act through them.

Leadership is the ability to present a vision so that others *want* to achieve it. It requires skills of building relationships with other people and organising resources effectively. Mastery of leadership is open to everyone.

The leader's tasks are to focus attention on a common purpose, to guide events and to organise activity. Cooperation among colleagues is inspired by encouraging a shared sense of purpose and an awareness of the importance of the task. It requires self-confidence to encourage others to complete assigned tasks, and to monitor progress while always highlighting a common vision.

A major source of this confidence is the respect which leaders have for themselves and other people. Ironically, those who already have a sense of inner worth receive respect and recognition from others naturally, while those who need to develop self worth receive little affirmation from others. They must start the process themselves.

This process of gaining self-respect can begin in everyday life when potential leaders make an effort to understand other peoples' difficulties. When colleagues' problems are sincerely acknowledged, mutual appreciation grows. This is the basis for giving and inevitably receiving respect.

There are leaders who gain power through bullying or manipulation. History and news stories from politics and business show repeatedly that this behaviour works in the short term only. Those leaders who inspire, build, create and encourage their colleagues have long-term success and are remembered long into the future. Those who undermine, destroy, cheat and belittle others are avoided as soon as their power begins to weaken – as it always does.

Self-assessment

One source of information about leadership effectiveness is feedback from other people. It is certainly a valuable exercise to discover the impact of leadership behaviour on colleagues. Occasionally, though, other people's remarks are biased, imprecise, or lack perception. How can a person identify which comments are useful and which are not? This question is particularly challenging because it is so tempting to disregard negative comments or adopt a defensive attitude to explain them away.

One answer to this problem is for leaders to assess their own performance first. This offers a baseline against which colleagues' comments, considered carefully, may be set. A strong self-image, clear goals for personal development and high performance standards help a leader to judge if comments are helpful, appropriate, or signal the need for a change in behaviour.

Obviously, self-assessment requires the strictest honesty. It is a waste of time and opportunity to create a fantasy self-image. Also, this process needs discrimination so that an assessment of *current* leadership skills is distinguished from *future* hopes for improved performance. By recognising the difference between 'who I am now' and 'who I want to be', leaders can produce a plan of action to achieve their goals for personal development.

Following the leader

All sorts of questions come to mind when embarking on
self-assessment:

- Am I fair?
- Do I take responsibility?
- Do I listen?
- Am I honest?
- Am I willing to debate?
- Do colleagues trust me?

The first challenge is to ask: 'Do I lead in such a way that I
would willingly follow myself?' Improved leadership
performance is based on a careful study of *actual* behaviour.
It helps to think of a recent leadership experience and then
focus on the details. Examining this specific performance
allows an assessment of leadership skill for that occasion.

Begin the process by listing five positive and five negative examples of *actual* and *current* leadership behaviour.

Positive leadership behaviour

1

2

3

4

5

Negative leadership behaviour

1

2

3

4

5

This total of 10 examples should readily come to mind. Fewer than 10 shows there is a strong need to develop better self-awareness. Alternatively, it could indicate a need for more leadership practice and experience. If either situation is the case, it is still of value to refer to the shorter list. Later, this activity should be repeated for other leadership experiences until the list includes at least 10 items.

The process of self-assessment can be continued next by considering colleagues' opinions and beliefs. Although this list depends upon guessing their reactions, it is useful to attempt it. There is always a benefit to be gained by trying to see the world from a colleague's point of view. Again, draw up two lists, one containing proposals of colleagues' positive opinions and beliefs, and one with their negative ideas.

Colleagues' positive beliefs

1
2
3
4
5

Colleagues' negative beliefs

1
2
3
4
5

Activity
- Compare the two lists: personal and colleagues' perceptions
- Are they the same throughout?
- If no, highlight the differences
- If yes, challenge yourself to try harder; then repeat the exercise
- How can you increase an awareness of your colleagues' perceptions?
- How can you increase self-awareness about your own performance?

Personal development

Assessment of both positive and negative leadership behaviour provides a basis for improving performance. Even so, any change in behaviour is best made so that it builds upon qualities which leaders actually possess and also enhances their natural personality. Everyone has a unique blend of qualities, such as courage, patience, ambition, honesty and others, and these core qualities are the real source of leadership success.

When these qualities are recognised, a leader can draw upon them with greater confidence. This also leads to discovery of which qualities leaders lack. With this information a leader can decide what needs to be developed and therefore how future performance can be improved.

For example, an inability to give clear directions is a negative leadership behaviour with a variety of potential causes. By examining their own personal make-up, individuals can identify the source of their difficulty. Do they need better preparation, more poise, tighter thinking or improved judgement? The same problem could require a different solution depending upon each person's blend of qualities and personal make up.

Positive behaviour
The first task is to identify this blend of individual qualities. The two lists of positive behaviour, drawn from personal and colleagues' points of view, aids this process. Each item on the lists potentially leads to identification of a personal quality.

For example, one item may read: 'Remained calm during a crisis'. This behaviour could result from a variety of qualities, such as courage, steadiness, trust, or others. When individuals recognise which quality is at the source of their calm, they can draw upon this consciously on future occasions. This insight has direct benefit for improving self-confidence. 'I am calm in a crisis because I have courage': this thought obviously enhances self-image. It also stabilises performance, because the quality is one which the individual already recognises and possesses.

Once a quality is identified for each item on the list, it is useful to write it next to that item. Some qualities may be repeated and others may offer a surprise. The point is that each feature of behaviour is drawn from a personal quality which in turn contributes to leadership performance. Frequently, this is difficult to believe or accept if any of these qualities has been criticised in the past.

For example, potential leaders who express gentleness, quiet or humility are not always understood. So rather than avoid expressing these qualities, leaders should learn how to present them so that they enhance the way they are seen as leaders. This is *always* possible, and the process begins with self-acceptance and a determination to explore how best to express each quality. Personal development means building upon existing strengths and managing weaknesses. Masking or hiding personal qualities creates good actors, not good leaders.

Negative behaviour

Negative comments provide further opportunity for growth. Through newly developed awareness, leaders can choose to change their behaviour. For example, if a leader is criticised for using humour when presenting official company business, this creates the possibility for choice. Options include deciding: that a sense of humour is not an appropriate leadership quality; that rebellion against the criticism and increased clowning activity is best; or that learning can be gained from the comment by discovering exactly what it means. Rather than react blindly, this individual can choose to analyse and grow.

On receiving negative feedback, leaders should ask:

- Did I really do what this person says I did?
- Does this person have all the facts?
- On reflection, do I believe my behaviour was appropriate to all three essentials: time, place and audience?
- If not, when, where and with whom is it appropriate to express this quality in this way?

Improving behaviour

Leaders who manage their behaviour effectively enhance their skills when leading others. Both positive and negative feedback offer valuable information and increased understanding about how behaviour impacts supporters. The lists of both positive and negative behaviour help to identify personal qualities. Negative items offer further benefit because they draw attention to specific behaviour which needs improvement.

In general, these items can be organised into three areas for development. These are: skills, knowledge and experience. On reviewing the lists of negative features, it can be asked of each item, 'Was this behaviour the result of a lack of skill, knowledge or experience?' Three lists can thus be compiled:

- *Skills*: list items which reveal a need for new skill
- *Knowledge*: list items which reveal a need for further knowledge
- *Experience*: list items which reveal a need for more experience

Plan of action

Developing skills, knowledge and experience strengthens the weak areas in leadership. Review the previous list of categorised features and decide which skills, knowledge and experience are necessary for leadership development, and then compile three lists:

- new skills
- new knowledge
- new experience

Next, consider how this development can be achieved in each of these three areas. Set one specific goal for each area:

- a goal for skills
- a goal for knowledge
- a goal for experience

Later, when these goals are achieved, the list can be reviewed again to set new goals for improving skills, knowledge and experience.

Checklist
- Think of one occasion, however great or small, during the day when you took the lead
- Describe this in one or two sentences
- What qualities did you express?
- What challenges did you experience?
- What do you like about your performance?
- What can you do to improve your performance?

Understanding people

The second step to successful leadership is understanding people. This means recognising individual differences in terms of drives, dreams and ambitions. There is a danger in believing that everyone is really the same. They are not, and it is not democratic to insist that they are. Differences, not similarities, make work groups strong and life interesting. When individuals are lumped together as 'the same', they are deprived of their independence and individuality.

Topics which are relevant to the development of this theme are:

- Motivation
- Rewards and values
- Inspiration

Motivation

Before the study of psychology gained social acceptance during this century, leaders generally kept silent about any feelings of self-doubt. Instead, they presented the world with an image of strength and determination and the appearance of complete confidence regardless of their inner state. The leader's task was 'to motivate others' through their example. Self-questioning was perceived to be a habit exclusively for weaklings. It even implied disloyalty and a lack of commitment to their position as leader.

Strength, determination and confidence continue to be valued leadership qualities. However, it is generally accepted now that leaders also experience a wide range of emotions and are driven by a variety of motives, some of which are positive and some negative. In fact, it is now considered a weakness to pose as the perfect and all-knowing leader. For example an admission of fear today is seen as a way to address and overcome it.

Managing negative as well as positive feelings requires an understanding of human motivation. One approach to this subject suggests that individuals are motivated to satisfy different needs at different times. Their first requirement is to meet their basic survival needs. Only when these are satisfied are they able to work towards achieving growth and creating meaning in their lives. It is the drive to fulfil needs for survival and growth which leads them to overcome feelings of fear and other limitations.

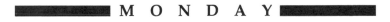

One pioneer in the study of human motivation is Abraham Maslow. He proposed that there is a hierarchy of needs with five different levels. As individuals satisfy all of the needs associated with each of these levels, they are then naturally drawn to progress and satisfy the needs on the next level. This idea suggests that human motivation is similar to the force which plants use to drive their roots through the hardest rock in search of nourishment. Maslow's hierarchy of needs is generally presented in the form of a pyramid as shown in the diagram below.

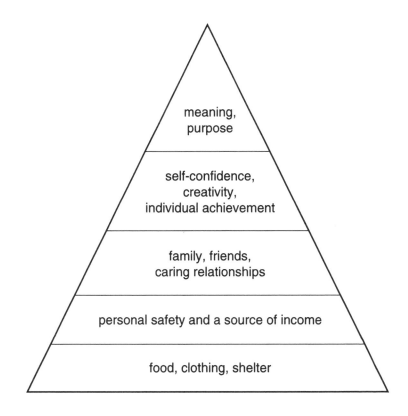

This model suggests that personal development follows a sequence. When immediate requirements of food, clothing and shelter are met, then individuals use their energy to ensure that their physical safety and comfort are secure in the future as well. Having satisfied these first two basic survival needs, they then give their full attention to building friendships and family relationships.

As soon as the need for belonging is satisfied, individuals then strive for a sense of personal achievement and an experience of self-esteem. Achieving satisfaction of all four of these need levels allows them to examine the purpose and meaning of their work and lives.

Essentially, this means that people who are hungry and without shelter give their primary attention to satisfying these needs before they feel willing or able to discuss philosophy. This also suggests that unsatisfied needs dominate behaviour. For example, a colleague who is under stress about money or is in poor health brings less attention to team relationships and certainly has impaired creativity.

Leaders benefit from discovering if there are special circumstances influencing performance. Even if they are powerless to help, they can show sensitivity when discussing performance issues and avoid taking a judgemental attitude.

The core idea is to understand the impact of needs on motivation and performance. This is the key to knowing how to play to colleagues' strengths and to help them overcome their weaknesses.

Motivation is never uniform throughout a whole team. A leader encourages team members to want to achieve team goals by recognising *each individual's* starting-point and building upon this. Inspirational speeches to the whole of the group at one extreme and punishment threats at the other have only a temporary influence on performance. Those measures which serve everyone in the long term focus on each colleague's driving concerns and issues. Satisfaction of *these needs* contributes directly to improved performance for the whole group.

Leadership practice
These checklists serve as a guide for applying Maslow's hierarchy of needs to understanding colleagues' motivation.

Think of a colleague with whom you work. What kinds of needs does this person discuss most?

- Physical comforts?
- Job security?
- Friends, family, social events?
- Job satisfaction, recognition, status?
- Values, principles, quality work for its own sake?

How does this person respond when issues related to each different level is raised?

- Easily and naturally?
- With a lack of comprehension?
- With impatience or cynicism?

If *easily and naturally*: these needs are likely to be satisfied on the level being discussed as well as on the levels below it.

If *lacking in comprehension*: it is likely that attention is focused more on satisfying needs on the level below.

If *impatiently and cynically*: needs are unlikely to be satisfied on this level or on the level below it. This has an impact on the person's overall ability to find satisfaction at work. Their motivation is affected because they assume they will be disappointed by what they receive.

Leadership solutions
When leaders understand the frustrations and limitations of their colleagues, they are better able *to present a vision so that others want to achieve it*. For example, when presenting the benefits of a quality improvement programme, it is less

effective to emphasise the importance of quality for its own sake when colleagues are primarily worried about losing their jobs.

Leaders who give proper attention to their colleagues' needs take time to explain that the quality programme not only benefits the company, but also contributes to each employee's work satisfaction, in terms of teamwork, job security and physical well-being. Addressing colleagues' concerns in this way shows respect for their needs and leads to increased motivation.

Rewards and values

During infancy and childhood, individuals form patterns of behaviour which ensure their survival. For example, some babies scream, cry and demand food and other essentials. Others babble, coo and charm their parents into giving them what they need. A third group simply learns that they are on their own and must expect the bare minimum from other people. Although actual behaviour changes with maturity, the underlying patterns remain in place.

These patterns of behaviour are in three categories. It is suggested that individuals tend to obtain what they need by using one of these patterns.

The three patterns are:

- Ambitious and assertive
- Caring and supportive
- Analytic and cautious

It is as if they have strong habits of behaviour often so powerful that they act as if they have no choice. Frequently, they are on 'automatic pilot' and are unaware of how they are behaving until a colleague comments upon it.

Even when leaders clearly explain that there are options, mental and behavioural habits lead the individual to act according to past patterns. Not only should leaders be aware of their own tendancies and personal pattern but they should also encourage colleagues to be more self-aware, particularly when their behaviour affects other people.

Ambitious and assertive
Ambitious and assertive individuals frequently have more ideas than there are hours in the day to achieve them. They are driven by a need to make their mark on the world. Recognising and supporting fulfilment of this need enables leaders to organise team tasks so that individuals can shine while achieving team priorities. This category of behaviour is an extremely challenging one to manage. Even so, when these individuals feel motivated to complete a task, nothing stops them.

Caring and supportive
Although the warmth and friendliness of these colleagues are certainly virtues, occasionally they result from a desire to please and be liked. Even so, they are a positive force in any group because these individuals truly enjoy giving support. In fact, they feel most rewarded when their help is accepted. The leader's task is to guide them towards becoming more independent and also to reassure them when the loners of the group refuse offers of their help.

Analytic and cautious

Analytic and cautious colleagues feel most satisfied when
they work alone. They enjoy the solitude, the concentration
and the sense of independence this gives them. For them to
complete the task is a reward in itself. For example, these
individuals genuinely feel burdened when asked to attend
an office party because it interferes with their work.

Properly managed, this pattern of behaviour is a valuable
asset to the team. It can bring depth to problem solving and
attention to complex questions. Unhappily, these loners
often find themselves with well-meaning leaders who are
determined to help them 'overcome their shyness'.

Here are some positive and negative features to each
pattern:

Ambitious and assertive

Positive features
- Confident
- Dynamic
- Risk-taking
- Spontaneous
- Directing
- Entrepreneurial
- Resourceful

Negative features
- Arrogant
- Pushy
- Gambling
- Impulsive
- Dictatorial
- Uncooperative
- Calculating

Caring and supportive

Positive features
- Sensitive
- Devoted
- Idealistic
- Friendly
- Tolerant
- Patient
- Understanding

Negative features
- Highly strung
- Doormat
- Deluded
- Naïve
- Blind
- Passive
- Submissive

Analytic and cautious

Positive features
- Practical
- Independent
- Fair
- Thorough
- Reserved
- Methodical
- Principled

Negative features
- Narrow-minded
- Self-serving
- Impersonal
- Nit-picking
- Isolated
- Plodding
- Rigid

- Circle both positive and negative words which you believe apply to yourself.
- When have you expressed this behaviour?
- Is any behaviour a habit?
- How does it help or hinder your leadership ability?

Inspiration

Shared understanding and sense of purpose provide a basis for strong relationships with leaders encouraging mutual respect between themselves and their supporters. However, there are still leaders who believe that it is necessary to set themselves apart from their followers. They believe that they need a mystique which is based upon their being different, more brilliant or better than their colleagues. They see this as their source of power.

Even 50 years ago this would have been considered conventional leadership behaviour, and yet now it is generally considered inappropriate. There has been an explosion of technology for information access through internet, intranet and telecommunications which subtly alters the way in which individuals relate to one another. Also, the average person is better educated and more sophisticated than the majority from previous generations. As a result, leaders are now required to manage people and information with greater flexibility and skill than ever before.

Successful leadership has always depended upon communication skills, both listening and speaking. There is now an additional need to use these skills to build interdependent relationships among group members and between the leader and the group. This doesn't dilute the role of leader; rather it adds new challenges.

In fact, it has always been a requirement of leaders to relate well to followers. History's greatest leaders show their awareness of this need by recognising that their authority and power emerged from their supporters.

The respect they gave their colleagues directly led to receipt of both loyalty and commitment. A major source of their ability to inspire emerged from the creation of positive relationships and mutual respect.

Checklist
- Think of one occasion during the day in which you took the lead
- Describe this in one or two sentences
- What did you want to achieve?
- Were there any personal needs which you were able to satisfy through leading?
- Were you aware of your colleagues' motivation?
- Did you consider their needs?
- Did your approach reflect a style which was ambitious and assertive, caring and supportive or analytic and cautious?

Power and authority

The third step to successful leadership refers to understanding issues of power and authority. When individuals accept the responsibility of leadership, they also assume the challenge of managing power wisely and for the benefit of their whole group. Topics which contribute to the right exercise of power and authority are:

- Managing power
- Styles of leadership
- Adapting to events
- Delegation

Managing power

The title 'leader' does not in itself create leadership. It has already been suggested that there should also be a positive relationship with those who are led. Discussion, feedback and debate are essential so that a leader can *learn* from other members of the group. Repressing, ignoring or discouraging different points of view within a group is a sign of a weak and frightened leader who is hiding behind a role in order to control the group.

At the heart of much of the debate about leadership style is the issue:

When leaders ask their colleagues for feedback, comments and advice, do they undermine or weaken their own authority?

Most definitely, they do *not*. Every leader potentially can be undermined, manipulated or overthrown. These hazards result more often from an *unwillingness to allow* debate, not from an openness to encourage it. Confidence, curiosity and tolerance are qualities of strong leadership. Inevitably, the leader who possesses these positive traits stimulates debate.

Only when everyone has had an opportunity to speak, does this leader recognise that it is time to bring the discussion to a close. A genuine interest in hearing colleagues' points of view and an open invitation to debate key issues is the mark of a powerful and confident leader, not a weak one.

Unfortunately, power is so often abused that for many it has become a dirty word. In fact, leaders who manage power effectively serve their organisations, colleagues and themselves. It is far better for people with integrity and character to assume positions of reponsibility than those who pursue power for its own sake.

There are four kinds of power exerted in most organisations. These are:

- Designated
- Expert
- Charismatic
- Information

Each contributes to successful leadership.

Designated power
This kind of power depends upon a specific and formally recognised organisational role. Individuals with this power are officially appointed to act on behalf of their organisations. When the role is left behind, the leader gives up the power associated with that role.

This means that a department head who vacates that position no longer has authority to lead. This passes to the next designated leader. On occasion, some leaders try to hang on to this kind of power; this behaviour creates considerable bad feeling and is never successful.

Expert power
This kind of power results from the personal talents, skills and experience of the individuals who possess it. They have this regardless of their official role within an organisation. Some leaders have both *designated* and *expert power* and find that the demands of their designated leadership role inhibit the development of the *highest* degree of expertise in their given field. This causes some specialists to avoid accepting

designated positions. Often, *expert power* is exerted informally. Effective leaders benefit the group when they cooperate with those who hold *expert power*.

Charismatic power
Those who have *charismatic power* possess both a blessing and a curse. They are frequently the 'wild cards' in any organisation. Historically, the highly charismatic are the leaders who tend to end up dead, in disgrace, alone in prison or in Hollywood!

Even so, a charismatic leader can certainly inspire colleagues to want to give their best, at least for a time. It is therefore tempting for these leaders to depend upon this kind of power as their sole source of influence. This is less than wise. To ensure that there is substance behind their charm and dazzle, leaders best draw on other sources of power *along with* charisma to influence events.

Information power
This source of power gains increasing importance because new electronic technology now allows the management of vast amounts of information. In the past, organisations depended upon long-serving staff to act as sources of *information power*. Human memory provided access to information which was vital and necessary for running the company. This is now more frequently available through electronic systems.

Because a lack of information at critical junctures is potentially catastrophic, this kind of power is best managed through sharing the responsibility for storing information.

In this way, the organisation avoids dependence upon single individuals and isolated electronic systems as sources of *information power*.

Integration
When leaders draw on more than one source of power, they strengthen their position. Exercising authority and influencing results becomes easier when the individual's source of power is obvious and is recognised immediately. There is a danger, of course, because it is very difficult to challenge a leader who draws authority from all four sources of power. On occasion even such a paragon will be wrong. This is reason enough to avoid becoming isolated or surrounded by 'yes-saying' admirers. This is a minimum safeguard against the mistaken use of power.

Activity
- Think of examples for all four kinds of power which you have observed being exercised
- Consider specific occasions when you have exercised each of these four kinds of power
- Is there any occasion when you chose to exercise the wrong kind of power (e.g. you overwhelmed colleagues with data when your task was to lead a meeting)?
- If you could relive this event, how would you manage power differently?

Styles of leadership

Power and authority are expressed through leadership style, and some writers propose there are three basic styles. These are:

- Democratic
- Autocratic
- Permissive

Democratic
A democratic style of leadership is based upon mutual respect among colleagues regardless of designated positions. When these leaders discover that their colleagues lack certain skills and abilities, they create opportunities for them to grow and develop. The strength of this style is the atmosphere of discussion and debate which it encourages.

Everyone gains from this, including the leaders who are

challenged to learn from their colleagues. There are few more satisfying leadership achievements than to gather a group of moderately skilled and underdeveloped colleagues and then, through working together, to create a team of individually powerful and dynamic peers.

In contrast, there are leaders who feel constantly frustrated because they are surrounded by witless underlings rather than peers. Even when they engage new people, these too gradually reveal their weakness. Such leaders are actually in serious trouble. When the whole world begins to look wrong, it is time to improve the viewer, not the viewed.

Autocratic

This style of leadership often appears to be most beneficial whenever there is controversy. Confused individuals long for a 'strong boss', a leader who will tell them what to do.

Certainly, there are enough historical examples of autocratic dictators who were *invited* into power to show that some people value this style of leadership very much.

However, there is strong research which suggests that groups with a single, order-giving leader, over the long term, suffer poorer productivity and performance as well as greater discontent than those who are led democratically. When leaders are too frightened, too proud or too conceited to open a discussion among their colleagues, they undermine their own authority. They have lost an opportunity to demonstrate their confidence, judgement and willingness to learn.

Permissive

The permissive style is frequently a misguided attempt at democracy. The individual who exercises this style of leadership is often well-meaning and reluctant to impose his or her will on other people. Unfortunately, these virtues can be infuriating to other people whose work requires coordination, active support and direction.

The permissive leader frequently does not realise that maintaining standards, giving guidance and acting as a forceful champion for the group is part of the leader's job. Although colleagues often like these 'nice guy' leaders – both male and female – they also describe them as weak, spineless and incompetent, regretting the day that they began working for them.

All three styles are both potentially beneficial and potentially frustrating to group members.

Frustrations
- *Democratic*: these leaders drive action-first colleagues crazy because discussion takes time and slows progress
- *Autocratic*: these leaders are so one-sided that they infuriate colleagues who want to contribute ideas and information
- *Permissive*: these leaders force their colleagues to accept inactivity through their avoidance of giving direction and guidance

Benefits
- *Democratic:* these leaders encourage everyone to contribute skills and talents so that more work of a higher quality gets done
- *Autocratic:* these leaders offer speed, single-mindedness and clarity when firm direction is required; there are occasions when a team actually benefits from being told what to do
- *Permissive:* these leaders best serve highly creative people who respond well to a structure-free environment. This style is useful when little group coordination is required

Adapting to events

Effective leaders are flexible when deciding which leadership style is the best one for their group at any given time. They determine this by considering the *stage of development* of their group. Two leading figures in the field of management study, Paul Hersey and Ken Blanchard, suggest that there are four distinct stages in the development of every group.

The *first stage* begins when the group first forms. The leader's role at this point should be directive so that the project gets under way. Once group members know their assignments and have clear directions, the leader next encourages them to get to know each other better. This builds strong group relationships and is the *second stage* of group development.

In the *third stage*, the leader emphasises the importance of members working well together, sharing responsibility and discussing the project's needs. In the *fourth stage*, the leader functions merely as a guide and coach to members, who begin to run the project themselves. Having passed through all four stages, they have grown into a mature group.

This four-stage model is very useful when deciding which leadership style is best for a group. It also helps explain why a group on occasion seems to benefit from being told what to do and at other times seems to resent it.

It is important to emphasise that the successful use of this model depends upon a leader's ability to assess a group's stage of development. An obvious challenge arises for the autocratic leader whose behaviour keeps the group from developing beyond stage one. This individual can easily argue that the model recommends directing and controlling activities because the group is still immature.

Delegation

The issue of group maturity is in part resolved if leaders also learn skills of delegation. There are four stages to this process as well. These are:

- Define the task
- Present why it is important
- Explain any expectations
- Evaluate and discuss results

Define the task
This is so obvious a step that it is often given little attention. Instead, an assignment is simply handed to a colleague who is then asked to get on with it. Leaders who want to ensure more reliable results take time to discuss the task in some detail by first asking their colleague how he or she would complete the assignment.

This uncovers questions and any gaps in that person's understanding. It also encourages comments and new ideas for the task's completion. This approach is essential to create *empowerment*, that is, encouraging a colleague to share in the responsibility for the task's completion and success. Inviting a discussion about the task when it is first assigned evokes a colleague's interest and stimulates commitment.

Present why it is important
Adults perform at their best when they see the relevance of what they are doing. They need a larger context in which to place a task or a project. This also further adds to their feeling of empowerment. When they know the significance

of the task they have been asked to perform, they can make better decisions about its completion and reduce their mistakes. Junior-level people appreciate information about context. It is a sign that the leader takes them seriously.

Explain any expectations

If colleagues do not know what is expected of them, they are seriously challenged to meet a leader's expectations. When delegating, it is essential to explain when and how they will be evaluated. People also need to know in advance any limitations upon their authority for completion of the task. Leaders who *say* that they give complete authority with the task cannot be surprised if this offer is accepted. Colleagues are not mind-readers. They cannot guess limits, even if these limits are completely obvious to the person delegating the task.

Evaluate and discuss results

This step builds upon the previous one. When expectations are explained in advance, then colleagues have clear performance goals towards which to work. When a leader reveals performance criteria only after a task is complete, this causes unnecessary hurt and disappointment. Also, it is virtually impossible to meet invisible or secret targets.

Keeping colleagues guessing is a leadership technique which belongs to the dark ages. There is no fairness in such a system of evaluation and it certainly undermines motivation for task completion. In essence, it is power-mongering, however cheerily or reasonably it is justified.

Checklist
- Think of one occasion during the day when you took the lead
- Describe this in one or two sentences
- What kind of power did you exercise?
- What alternative kinds of power would also have served this situation?
- What style of leadership did you use?
- How did your colleagues respond to your leadership?
- What stage of development has your group achieved?
- Were there any tasks which you could have delegated today but did not?
- What were these tasks and how will you delegate them next time?

Communication

All of work and social exchange depends upon communication. It is *the* means for sharing ideas, feelings and resources. When communication breaks down, disagreements and misunderstandings immediately occur. Even so, communication skills are frequently taken for granted.

It is assumed that colleagues who speak the same language need only time, effort and sincerity to communicate successfully. This optimistic view ignores the impact of emotions, motivation, intelligence, risk-taking and competition – among many other issues. For this reason, communication is the fourth step to successful leadership and includes these essential topics:

- Listening and speaking
- Social skills
- Creating understanding

Listening and speaking

Communication is based upon giving and receiving information. In its simplest form, this consists of two activities: listening and speaking. In fact, both of these require highly complex behaviour and draw upon an individual's lifetime of experience.

Even a brief encounter consisting of only a casual greeting is the result of years of practice. Through trial and error over the passage of time, individuals create a personal style of greeting and become so skilled that they also know how to adapt this to meet the changing needs of each situation.

Listening
Listening requires a leader to be aware of three essential features: bias, visual signals and vocal sounds.

1 Bias Everyone's point of view includes some bias even if this is not entirely conscious. Bias is a way of thinking which colours a point of view about a person, event or idea and influences a person's ability to understand and interpret correctly what they see and hear. A basic challenge is to identify the extent to which bias undermines good judgement or the ability to hear accurately what is said.

Bias is a problem when it seriously distorts an individual's understanding. It becomes dangerous when it also limits the ability to recognise when it exists or that it has a negative influence. One result of bias is the exclusion of information whose source is unattractive or in some way different from the listener.

Indicators of bias include extreme reactions to people or situations, either in favour or against; paying attention only to the parts of a presentation which are already understood; or assuming an understanding of what is said before a statement is even finished.

2 Visual signals   A visual sign is body language. There are many seminars and books available which offer interpretations of commonly used gestures and signs. These often represent a sincere effort to improve understanding and communication. However, in a multicultural society, it should also be emphasised that gestures carry a wide variety of meanings for different cultural groups.

People interpret the meaning of body language according to their own understanding. A population with diverse backgrounds and nationalities lacks a common meaning for the symbols contained in visual language. Therefore it is unwise to make generalisations about a *single meaning* for certain signs and gestures as if there were a universal code available.

However, gestures add considerable meaning to communication. Listening is obviously enhanced when both eyes and ears are used simultaneously. The difficulty is assuming that there is an understanding when there is a possibility of doubt. If a speaker depends upon ambiguous gestures, then it is important to ask what these mean. An incorrect interpretation of visual signals can lead to serious misunderstanding.

3 Vocal sounds Listening to the sound and tone of a speaker's voice helps understanding. Sometimes there are hidden messages which are heard with careful listening. For example, speakers signal their emotional state as well as an attitude towards their audience through their voice. At times, it is more important to hear these subtle messages than the actual content of what is said. If a speaker's tone of voice contrasts with the actual spoken message, then a listener should ask for clarification. Although this requires tact, it contributes to improved understanding.

Activity
- During the day, please observe at least three conversations between people you do not know.

Conversation one: Bias
- Do you imagine that there is any bias between these people?
- What causes you to think this?
- If you were engaged in this conversation, would you experience any bias?
- What form do you imagine this would take?
- What could you do about your own bias in order to improve understanding?

Conversation two: Visual signals
- Do these people seem to share a cultural background?
- Are they using similar gestures and facial expressions?
- How and when are these signals used?
- Do you understand their significance?
- How do you know that you understand?
- What could you do to improve your ability to interpret these visual signals?

Conversation three: Vocal signals
- Does the tone of voice match the content of what is being said?
- Do both speakers use the same voice tone and volume?
- Do they seem aware of the impact of their voice tone on the other person?
- If you joined this conversation, would you use a similar tone of voice?
- What could you do to become more conscious of the effect of your voice on others?

Speaking

From the lightest social conversation to the most challenging business exchange, speaking requires an ordered and logical presentation of ideas. Although speaking activity is frequently taken for granted, it is improved by preparation. In many cases, this preparation is so rapidly achieved that speaking occurs simultaneously as an individual plans what is to be said.

This style is called 'flying by the seat of your pants', 'thinking on your feet' or 'winging it'. Much is left to chance when speakers depend solely upon this approach. The most effective speakers use techniques which make listening to them an easy and positive experience. These techniques include: headlining, pacing and summarising.

1 Headlining   Just as a news headline signals a story's main ideas, speakers can highlight their key thoughts in their opening sentence. They begin by stating clearly what they want to discuss and then expanding upon this initial idea. When each main thought is completed, they then give another headline. This approach avoids listeners having to ask: 'What is the point?' If this has *ever* happened to a speaker, even once, then this technique is a useful one to develop.

2 Pacing   Good speakers attend to the needs of their audience. Pacing refers to the ability to stop talking and invite listeners to comment. Sadly, some speakers believe that their turn to speak is over only when they have expressed every one of their ideas. Too often this also means exhausting their audience as well.

An alternative approach suggests that a speaker pauses when presentation of each headline is complete. The listener then responds or offers a new headline. Both speakers and listeners contribute actively and participate equally when using this approach.

Pacing also refers to a speaker's ability to create interest by slowing and speeding up delivery of a message. Speakers who use a single tone of voice without changing its rhythm are less engaging than those with a more variable style.

3 Summarising 'I tell them what I plan to say; then I tell them; then I tell them what I just said.' This is the age-old wisdom for report-writing and public speaking. It is a belt-and-braces approach not entirely suitable for everyday conversation, but it does highlight the importance of summarising key ideas. Gathering several headlined ideas into a summary adds structure to communication. It signals that there is mutual understanding – or at least that certain points have been discussed and are complete.

Activity
- During three separate conversations, please practice these three techniques.

Conversation one: Headlining
- Before beginning to speak capture your main thought in a headline
- Begin by stating the headline clearly and briefly
- Continue speaking so that you expand upon this headline *only*

- If other related issues emerge, make headlines for each of these
- Be aware of moving from one headline to another

Conversation two: Pacing
- Listen and identify the pace of the other person
- As you speak, notice if your pace is different
- Alter your pace if you can without losing the thread of what you are saying
- Be aware of the signals you use to show that you have finished speaking
- Be aware of the signals the other person uses to show a wish to speak

Conversation three: Summarising
- When you complete a headline, paraphrase what has been said
- After several contributions by both speakers, highlight key points
- When the discussion has slowed, make a clear statement of its conclusions so far
- At the end of the conversation, list all of the headlines which were covered

Social skills

Listening and speaking form the foundations of communication. They both contribute in equal measure to the development of socially skilled information exchange. Researchers highlight five essential features of clear and effective communication and refer to them as social skills. Socially skilled communication is:

- Goal-directed
- Coherent
- Appropriate to the situation
- Controlled
- Able to be learned

Goal-directed

When there are clear goals for the exchange of ideas or information, it is easier to recognise when communication is complete. Discussion is far more satisfying when participants have something they wish to achieve through communication because they can then work to accomplish this.

Telling a joke is an excellent example of goal-directed communication. The narrator knows the communication is successfully completed when the listener starts to laugh.

Taking time to consider the purpose of sharing information influences the choice of words and contributes to a more confident presentation.

Coherent

This refers to behaviour which makes a single, consistent overall impression as well as to the clarity and logic of the message. For example, when presenting serious information that could alarm a listener, a socially skilled speaker controls eye contact, facial expression, tone of voice and body language so that they blend to give a single message. Nervous smiling or a hesitating manner when information is urgent detracts from the speaker's credibility and potentially distorts the message.

Appropriate to the situation

Socially skilled communication coordinates words, behaviour and timing so that presentation of information matches the needs of the situation. While coherence refers specifically to *personal style* when delivering a message, this additional skill requires thinking about when and how a message is best delivered. This means choosing the right method, such as telephone, handwritten note, electronic means or face-to-face speech. One example of this social skill is a leader who criticises a colleague face to face in private rather than in a public place.

Controlled

This social skill refers to the leader's self-discipline rather than the ability to discipline others. On occasion, leaders make decisions which benefit the group rather than reflect their personal preference.

An example of this kind of behaviour is the leader who resists taking over a task once it has been delegated. It takes enormous control to watch a younger colleague struggle to learn a task which the leader could complete in just a few minutes. The reward for this kind of self-control is a stronger team. Control in this example means choosing to be silent.

Able to be learned
The ability to learn is a vital social skill and most communication behaviour is learned by absorption and copying rather than by conscious choice. A speaker's voice, gestures and movement are the end result of a lifetime of conditioning. Leaders can improve these skills when they evaluate their own performance towards discovering new ways to express themselves.

This process is aided by examining the strength of the other four social skills. When there is a gap in the ability to set a goal for discussion, to be coherent, to time the delivery of information, or to maintain self-control, then leaders need to focus attention on social skill development.

Preparation for an important communication
- What are your goals for this occasion, both personal and professional?
- Does your style of dress, choice of language and tone of voice make a single, harmonious impression?
- Is the timing and choice of method right for the delivery of your message?

- Are you as fully prepared to listen to others as you are to speak?
- What do you plan to learn from this experience?

Creating understanding

It is the leader's responsibility to open a debate, encourage colleagues' contributions and guide discussion so that a common understanding emerges within the group. This understanding enhances a group's sense of purpose and contributes to their sense of unity.

Opening a discussion which addresses difficult issues offers an enormous challenge. Some leaders just give up at the first sign of dissent or confusion. They begin to bark orders and silence discussion out of fear of losing control. However, if they could develop the courage to persevere, they would reap enormous rewards.

When leaders are committed to creating understanding, they show this through attentive listening and setting a tone of tolerant discussion within the group. Not only do these leaders gain benefit from their colleagues' ideas, they also encourage group loyalty and commitment. It has already been suggested that respect generates respect. The leader has the power to begin this positive spiral of mutual appreciation.

The key task is to achieve a balance between creative contribution and opinion free-for-all, where the loudest voice gets heard most. To avoid anarchy while also fostering debate requires a leader to set and follow ground rules for the discussion. These ensure that everyone's ideas receive a fair hearing. The leader assumes the role of discussion moderator. This is a difficult task although skilled practitioners make it look very easy. The goal is to encourage a free exchange among all and avoid domination by just a few.

Discussion skills include:

- Coaching
- Paraphrasing
- Intervention

Coaching

An essential leadership task is to state the purpose for the discussion at the beginning. If this is an open debate, then one person must not be allowed to hold forth and dominate. To avoid this as the discussion begins, the leader should announce that people should speak one at a time and wait to be acknowledged for their turn.

As the discussion continues, the leader watches who in the group wants to speak. A system of turn-taking should be followed during even an informal gathering. Some leaders fail to monitor discussion in this way, arguing that they want to avoid 'controlling' the debate. As a result, some participants speak up when they wish and others hold back or are spoken over. Forced silence creates frustration. Avoiding responsibility for monitoring the debate, shows a permissive leadership style.

This is always unsatisfactory and allows the loudest and most confident to control the discussion. It is better to risk insisting that forceful members wait for acknowledgement than to ignore the quiet participants. A fair leadership style during discussion earns everyone's respect and encourages full participation. Even highly vocal members eventually appreciate fairness.

Paraphrasing
If the discussion digresses from the main point, paraphrasing allows the leader to bring it back on track. This requires repeating the key ideas of the side topic in summary form and then linking this to what has been covered on the main topic. This is best accomplished in a non-judgmental manner.

If leaders catch digression quickly, they avoid feelings of frustration themselves and can more easily reaffirm the main topic without showing any strain. Those who began the digression can be invited to raise their points again when discussion of the main topic is concluded.

Intervention

When two or more participants are locked in a dispute, they need encouragement to pause and take a step back from their positions. This is so that they can gain a new perspective. It then helps to ask the other participants to speak on the issue under dispute. If a new voice takes this opportunity to raise a different topic, the leader should gently insist on staying with the controversial issue. A change of topic leads to continuation of a dispute rather than resolution.

Occasionally, a well-meaning participant tries to change the discussion topic as a way of avoiding controversy. Skilful intervention does not allow this to happen. The leader's task is to take attention away from the disputing *participants* and focus on the *issues* which they raised. The next step is to encourage the rest of the group to discuss the controversial issues towards finding a solution.

Checklist

- What did you learn from the three observed conversations which focused on listening?
- What did you learn from the three observed conversations which focused on speaking?
- Think of an occasion during the day when you took the lead to communicate ideas
- Describe this in one or two sentences
- Did you have a goal, either personal or professional, for your communication?
- How do you rate your performance in terms of:
  - coherence?
  - appropriateness?
  - self-control?
- At any time during the day, did you lead a group discussion?
- If so, how do you rate your ability to:
  - coach?
  - paraphrase?
  - intervene?

Decision-making

The fourth step for successful leadership is decision-making. Whether leaders do this alone or within a group, it is essential that they act with confidence. Further, when the discussion of a decision is complete, it is the leader who signals that it is time to take action. Decision-making skills are improved by focusing on these issues:

- What are priorities?
- Setting clear goals
- A systematic approach

What are priorities?

Frequently, leaders are required to make several decisions at the same time. Because full attention cannot be given to each issue simultaneously, they need to coordinate and manage information with considerable skill. There are also added distractions because many of their decisions have unforeseen impact upon other matters. Decision-makers must determine the extent of interdependence among a variety of issues even as they are estimating their degree of importance.

This requires identifying priorities and making decisions about the most pressing issues first. This takes discipline, because some decisions appear to require immediate attention and yet lack genuine urgency or importance for the long term. Alternatively, some truly vital issues may be delayed or even forgotten because they lack glamour or enough noisy advocates to press for their attention.

Priorities have two features: *urgency* and *importance.* The leader's task is to identify these and act upon them.

Complications also occur when urgent but not important issues demand time and attention. Leaders are then required to make further decisions even while coordinating previously identified priorities. With practice, the juggling act which attends managing priorities and making timely decisions becomes a routine performance.

The process of acquiring these skills begins with knowing how to recognise priorities. Confusion can arise because some tasks are urgent and yet of only short-term relevance. For example, assigning a staff member to give a group of school children a tour of the building is of limited relevance to the business. Even so, it is an urgent matter if the school children are standing in the cold waiting to be invited indoors.

Two criteria
When prioritising decisions, it is useful to separate issues into 'important' and 'urgent'. Some decisions fit neither category, while others fit both. A few urgent decisions are also highly important because they provide a basis for future decisions. For example, a deadline for action gives urgency to the decision to file a request to the town council for planning permission. Although the actual decision to complete the form is a minor one, it has long-term

importance as well because it marks the first step for major decision-making later.

Priority setting begins by examining all of the decisions which are currently required of the leader and the group. These can be listed in preparation for discussion by the whole group or for study by an individual or a small working party.

To illustrate this, the manager of a 10-member accounts department reviews several forthcoming decisions. These could include office refurbishment, holiday schedules, staff allocation for new projects and a new insurance benefits package proposed by the company's personnel officer.

Each of these main issues includes sub-tasks which will contribute to completion of the larger task. Even so, the manager wants to avoid getting drawn into considering the details of each decision before assessing the urgency and importance of the four main topics. Time is particularly tight for this leader and so knowing which decisions are both urgent and important is essential. By setting priorities, decision-making time can be better managed.

The four issues are listed on a tally sheet. Each issue can then be quickly assessed for its urgency and importance. This tally sheet also helps to organise and assess decision-making for the sub-tasks as well.

Tally of items	Urgent	Important
Office refurbishment	no	no
Holiday schedules	yes	no
Staff allocation	yes	yes
Insurance benefits	no	yes

In the tally illustrated here, the manager believes that office refurbishment is neither urgent nor important in the long-term. Although there is money budgeted for this project and much discussion about colours and materials has occurred, the proposal originated at the company's headquarters 300 miles away. Staff are enthusiastic but are also happy with their office as it is. This is also the department's busiest season and they are all feeling highly pressured by their work requirements.

The next item, holiday schedules, is an urgent matter for the short term because staff need to make holiday plans with their families. Even so, the actual schedule of dates does not have long-term significance for the department. As long as everyone receives their fair amount of holiday time and their family needs are given consideration, the staff are usually well satisfied.

On the other hand, staff allocation for new project work is not only urgent but also has long-term importance to the department. Several projects are now almost complete and new assignments must be given in advance to allow initial preparation to occur. This decision is also extremely important because skilful scheduling has a direct impact on departmental productivity and the overall budget.

The decision about the insurance benefits package is not due for several weeks. Although the staff have received the background information on the available options, it is unlikely that they have all read it thoroughly as yet. This is necessary because the final decision will lock the department into a single package of health care for an indefinite period. This isn't a decision to be taken lightly or quickly. Even so, it is enough at this stage to remind staff that the deadline for a decision is in another month.

After tallying the list of issues, it becomes obvious that attention should be given first to the work allocation issue because this decision is both urgent and important. Because holiday schedules are also urgent, these should be addressed immediately as well. In fact, all of the information gathered for the new work schedules also serves the task of organising holiday leave. These two urgent tasks can readily be completed in coordination.

In contrast, the office refurbishment is a low priority in terms of both urgency and importance and so it should be delayed until the department's work load slows down. Although its enthusiasts are likely to understand this, presentation of the tally makes a convincing case for postponement.

Activity
- Make a list of issues which require you to make a decision
- Which items on the list are sub-tasks of a larger issue?
- Which are main issues?
- Organise the list so that it highlights the main tasks. Sub-tasks should be grouped under each main task

- Notice if any sub-tasks contribute to completion of more than one main issue. Put a star next to these items
- Assess the identified main tasks on a tally sheet on the model used in the example above.

Setting clear goals

Identification of priorities allows leaders to focus on the urgent and important decisions first. The successful outcome of these decisions then depends upon setting clear goals. This can seem an obvious point because the priority itself would seemingly provide the goal. However, goals at the outset of a decision-making process are often too vague and general to give sufficient direction.

To illustrate this challenge, the office refurbishment item from the previous section offers a useful example. The decision 'office refurbishment' can be interpreted in a variety of ways. It could mean new paint, carpets and furniture. Sub-tasks as a result would include choice of colour schemes, materials and layout design. The decision could alternatively mean a complete physical overhaul in order to prepare for future *intelligent building* installations.

Clarity about the desired end result for 'office refurbishment' guides the development of goals towards achieving this. Clearly stated goals allow a group of decision-makers 'to speak the same language'. Much decision-making time is wasted because individuals lack a shared understanding of what specifically is required of their decision. Options are therefore proposed, discussed, selected or rejected in an almost random fashion as decision-makers speak at cross-purposes.

Alternatively, when a desired end result is clearly stated and understood, decision-makers can more easily plan a course of action to achieve the goal. Goals give decision-makers a standard against which they can evaluate planning options. The choice which best serves their goal is the one which is the most appropriate.

> A goal is a general and realistic aim for achievement. In decision-making, it makes explicit the requirements and the desired end result for the decision.

Goals give direction to the decision-making process. Even so, the need to achieve a specific outcome must also be balanced with a flexible attitude. On occasion, overly high expectations or rigid criteria limit success.

Defining goals
The following are examples of business related issues requiring decisions.

> - To raise the company's profile in the community
> - To reduce customer complaints by 10 per cent
> - To purchase a two-acre piece of land adjoining the company's current headquarters

These statements are all types of goals providing a varying degree of detail. The way a goal is phrased influences the way it is discussed.

The first goal is the most general. It is a useful style of goal when beginning a decision-making discussion. It states in general terms a desired end result so that participants are invited to generate a variety of solution options. These options can then be examined individually.

As the discussion continues, the decision-makers become clearer about what they want to achieve and so they are able to narrow the focus of their debate. For example, options which could be generated 'to raise the company's profile' could include:

- Sponsoring a marathon
- Getting press coverage for community service projects
- A director joining the local school board

As each option is discussed, decision-makers discover they have varying interpretations of 'profile in the community'. This enables them to reach better agreement about what they want and the goals they should set.

The second goal is more specific because it includes an exact measurement for the decrease in complaints. Any option which fails to meet this criterion could then be readily eliminated. When a specific quantity or precise detail is included in a decision-making goal, there should be a strong reason. Details enhance the goal *only* if they are valid and necessary. Otherwise, beneficial options which do not provide the exact outcome could be eliminated unnecessarily.

The third goal is very specific. It limits decision-making to those options which meet its several precise criteria. This kind of goal serves decision-makers who have already determined *what* they need to do. Their next step is to generate options in order to decide *how* they intend to achieve this.

State intentions
Goal-setting is an important step in the decision-making process. It can be used to generate new options or to narrow the focus and eliminate less appropriate options. When formulating goals, decision-makers should make explicit what they want to achieve through their discussion. The more important the decision, the more time is required. Even so, misunderstanding is limited when decision-makers realise that goals can serve different purposes at different stages of the decision-making process.

SO, NO BEATING ABOUT THE BUSH —
SOMEBODY DEFINITELY OUGHT TO
DO SOMETHING, AND
SOONISH

A systematic approach

There are always risks involved in decision-making. The most obvious is selection of the wrong choice. Hidden forces and unforeseen circumstances can undermine the best of decisions. Even so, a careful study of all available information leads to more effective decisions.

Testing the options
One method of decision-making begins with a thorough analysis of all of the available options. This process reveals the relative merits of each proposed course of action. Having defined a goal – that is, the desired end result of the decision – the next step is to distinguish the essential or *primary* requirements from any *secondary* requirements. This provides a means for weighing the merits of each choice.

Making a decision about a holiday destination provides a good example of this process. There are often real constraints in terms of timing, costs and method of travel which provide examples of primary requirements. Certain criteria are actually so important that failure to meet them means cancellation of the holiday. For example, the following three features are the *primary requirements* for two individuals who decide to holiday together.

Primary
- Seven days available
- £800 maximum budget
- Warm and sunny climate

In addition to these primary features, they also have some secondary requirements associated with their decision. Although these criteria are important to them as well, they are not as critical as the primary requirements. Their secondary requirements are as follows.

Secondary
- Resort on the beach
- Travel and hotel package is available
- Location popular to peers
- Active social and night life
- Comfortable transport and journey
- Stable exchange rate
- Their native language is widely spoken

Another tally sheet helps to organise all of the available information.

Desired end result: to take a fun-centred holiday away from home

	A Florida World	B La Plage Pleasure	C Costa Fabula
Primary requirements			
1 Seven days available	2 days' travel	1 day's travel	1 day's travel
2 £800 maximum	£1100	£795	£750
3 Warm and sunny climate	–	yes	yes

The desired end result is to have a fun-centred holiday away from home. This makes explicit that the holiday should provide relaxation as well as a break from routine. Therefore destinations which offer 'educational opportunities' or 'job-related contacts' are not options. Clarity at this initial stage about the decision-makers' intentions reduces potential for any confusion and bad feeling later.

In this example, there are three possible destinations, all of which have been highly recommended to the two decision-makers. Each of these destinatons is listed across the top row in columns A to C. The primary requirements are listed down the column on the left side of the page.

Next, each of the destinations should be tested against the primary requirements. As soon as an option fails, it is disqualified. Occasionally, decision-makers reveal that they have an attachment to one of the options by saying, 'Well, perhaps I can be flexible about that feature after all.' This means that it *was not* a primary requirement and should be added to the list of secondary requirements instead. *Primary* is exactly that: if the option does not meet this feature then it fails the decision's requirements and is disqualified.

Option A is Florida World. Travel from their home requires an entire day each way. This would still allow five days in the resort and so this option just barely passes. Even so, the holiday costs £1100 as a minimum figure and so it is too expensive. Although the decision-makers hesitate a bit, they realise that this feature effectively disqualifies this option.

...OR THERE'S ALWAYS OPTION 4 — A SUNRAY LAMP AND A POTTED PALM

Option B is La Plage Pleasure. Travel is less than a half of a day each way. It costs less than £800 and the climate there is always sunny and warm. Because it meets all three criteria, it remains an option. This is also true of Costa Fabula. This process leaves two options for final consideration. Now the secondary requirements must be considered.

Secondary requirements	B	C
1 Resort on the beach	10	8
2 Travel and hotel package	7	7
3 Location popular to peers	9	9
4 Active social and night life	9	9
5 Comfortable transport and journey	10	7
6 Stable exchange rate	9	5
7 Native language widely spoken	7	9
Total	61	54

When the decision-makers first made this list of secondary requirements, they thoroughly discussed what was most important to them about the holiday. This makes it easier for them to complete the rest of the tally. They now give a score to each of their options in terms of how well they match the secondary requirements.

Each requirement can receive a maximum score of ten points so that if the option matches the requirement exactly, then it should receive all ten points. For example, option B is located on a clean and sandy beach. Therefore it gets all ten points. Option C is located along the side of a harbour and is a five-minute walk away from the beach. Although it is 'ocean side', it gets only eight points because it doesn't entirely match the requirement.

The decision-makers proceed to score the options against each of the other six features, estimating how closely each matches the requirement. When this process is completed, they total the scores. In this case, option B is clear winner. Also, the decision-makers have had a chance to discuss their holiday priorities thoroughly through scoring each feature together. When the final decision is made to go to La Plage Pleasure, they both feel that they took an active part in the process.

Applications
This method is particularly useful when there is controversy over the available options. A leader in this case would first guide the discussion towards identifying the primary and secondary requirements. This gives a structure to the debate and allows those who are involved in the decision to express their views more easily.

An additional step

For many decisions, the secondary requirements each have a different 'weight', that is, some are more important to a successful outcome than others. When this is the case, an additional step should be added to the tally process. Each secondary requirement should be assigned a weight from one to ten to show that requirement's 'importance'.

Next, each option should be scored as described before from one to ten to show the degree to which it matches each requirement. This time, though, this score should be multiplied by each requirement's weight of 'importance'. When the 'importance' rating is included, an option's overall score can be changed dramatically.

For example, the 'importance' score for the sixth requirement on the list could be set at nine because it controls their available spending money. Option B is located in a country with a stable exchange rate and so it receives a score of nine. When this is multiplied by the 'importance' score of nine, this equals 81 points. Option C is located in a country with a less stable rate of exchange and so it receives only five points. When this is also multiplied by nine, it becomes 45 points.

Alternatively, if the requirement's 'importance' is given only a weight of two, then option B would receive 18 points (a score of nine multiplied by an 'importance' of two) and C would have 10 points (a score of five multiplied by an 'importance' of two). The benefit of including 'importance' in the scoring is revealed when a comparison is made of the requirement's scores. If the requirement has an 'importance' of nine, option B has a score of 81 points versus 45 points for option C. An 'importance' of two would have a score of 18 versus 10.

Checklist
- Think of one occasion during the day when you made a decision
- Describe this in one or two sentences
- Did you have a clear sense of the decision's priority?
- If so, how did you determine this?
- How readily did you distinguish between urgency and long-term importance?
- Did you have a thorough understanding of the purpose your decision should serve?
- If not, how could you improve that understanding?

Creating a vision

Vision is the distant light which gives direction to any effort. When this is clear and bright, it attracts attention and stimulates curiosity and interest. Even when the details are vague or indistinct, they serve as a reminder that there is more to life than the routine and ordinary. Leaders who offer vision to their colleagues inspire at least as much determined action as those who promise money, status and influence.

When leaders express vision in a way which touches their supporters, they invite strong commitment. Vision provides the common purpose which leads to united action. Creating a vision is the sixth step for successful leadership and it is a crucial one. Topics which contribute to an understanding of this theme are as follows:

- Vision and purpose
- The big picture
- Framing and reframing

Vision and purpose

In general, visionaries are not the most comfortable kind of people to be around. Particularly if their ideas differ dramatically from the conventional view, they are judged by the world to be nutters, fanatics or freaks. Extremes of thinking often seem too unusual for wide acceptance. The determined visionary occasionally contributes to this negative reaction by behaving in an eccentric way.

However, it is vision, not the behaviour of the visionary, which transforms an ordinary manager or administrator into a leader. Vision suggests that it is possible to make things better and this is inspiring. Let us return to the definition of leadership presented in the first step of this development programme:

Leadership is the ability to present a vision so that others *want* to achieve it. It requires skills of building relationships with other people and organising resources effectively. Mastery of leadership is open to everyone.

As an alternative to this, managers and administrators present ideas, proposals, memos and suggestions. They can demand, insist, direct, convince and even encourage their colleagues to cooperate. Depending upon their degree of power and influence, they can also be assured of success. While effective management deserves both praise and reward, it is not leadership.

Leaders have vision, take risks, present dreams, explore possibilities and in general invite their colleagues to join them for a journey into the unknown. Managers have reports, analyse data and ask their colleagues to meet them in the conference room after lunch. Even when leaders blend perfectly into their organisational surroundings, there is something just a little bit different about them. On close examination, that 'something' is often vision.

Activity
- Close your eyes and ask yourself to what degree do you actually achieve your full potential – personally as well as professionally
- What new feature, behaviour or activity would enhance your life – personally as well as professionally?
- What would symbolise this addition in terms of a single word, an object or an image?
- What would you like your future to be like – personally as well as professionally?
- Is there any image or situation which summarises this dream?

This activity begins the process of developing a personal sense of vision. Whenever individuals lift their attention from routine matters, they open themselves up to new possibilities. The ability to envision, to imagine something new and better, to dream, can be acquired with practice. The necessary effort is worthwhile because vision is an essential ingredient of leadership.

Even so, the decision to be a leader rather than a perfectly adequate boss or manager should not be taken lightly. The front line is far more dangerous than the back. Both the demands and the challenges of leadership are far greater than those of routine administration. It has already been suggested that the presenters of vision are not always comfortable people. They are also not always popular.

Leadership requires a high degree of personal commitment and the loss of much personal choice. The glamour of presenting a vision doesn't soften the blow if it is rejected or is widely misunderstood. This experience is far more painful for a leader than the refusal of a proposal, idea or working paper for a manager. Leaders by definition have the kind of relationship with their supporters which makes them more vulnerable to their reactions. However tough or 'macho' some leaders may appear, is it *really* possible for anyone to avoid feeling hurt when their most deeply felt ideas are rejected?

Leaders who are aware of this danger create stability for themselves through feeling confident that they are *truly* the right choice for their position. They achieve this because they know it is their unique blend of personal qualities which calls them to serve their group at this time. Their sense of vision has guided them to consider carefully the purpose they serve through leadership. Although vision creates vulnerability, it also provides an immense source of strength when under fire.

The big picture

Courage in the face of adversity is one of the more inspiring leadership qualities. Like the hero in an action film, a leader in times of crisis needs to believe in the possibility of a positive outcome to each conflict, problem or challenge. Leaders more than anyone else are in charge of promoting the belief in a happy ending, even if this seems only the remotest possibility.

'Big picture thinking' allows them to achieve this with credibility. This refers to the ability to shift attention from the details of an immediate situation to see how these fit into the bigger picture.

In this way leaders gain fresh perspective and often find new solutions to nagging problems. Thinking in terms of the bigger picture focuses on these relationships so that a new image appears. This often gives leaders new insight and the ability to find new solutions.

For example, a request to a department to cut its expenses could be viewed as part of a bigger picture of the company's finances. This could show that the company is facing a loss if its costs are not reduced. The decision to ask a department to cut expenses could be the result of a wish to avoid making staff redundant.

The bigger picture highlights the possibility of a positive outcome in this case. On occasion, big picture thinking can reveal hidden threats or potential weaknesses. Leaders are then able to take action before difficulties arise.

The big picture offers a view of a company or group as a whole. Artificial divisions fall away when people and events appear in a larger context. Sometimes this is called 'helicopter viewing': that is, 'going up' mentally to examine the whole of an area of activity. This perspective emphasises patterns of behaviour and draws attention to anything which doesn't fit.

Activity

1 Focus attention on one observed interaction between two or three people
2 How would you describe the interaction in terms of:
   • the possible purpose for the contact?
   • the potential outcome for each person as a result of the contact?
   • any underlying emotions, positive or negative?
   • any expressed emotion, positive or negative?
3 Now, imagine that there is a cable attached to each person in this exchange. Mentally follow each of these cables to trace all of the activity which led to the observed interaction
4 These activities contribute to the bigger picture for this interaction
5 Once you develop this bigger picture, reconsider the list of questions included in the above item 2

Framing and reframing

In the dictionary, framing is defined as 'an established order or system, or the way that a thing may be constructed, organised or formed'. It is also a term used to describe the *habits of mind* which people develop to view and interpret the world. This topic is touched upon in Wednesday's section on bias, because rigid frames of reference contribute to the creation of biased thinking.

Each person 'frames' the world in a unique way, so that two people who witness the same events may interpret them differently. Frames are based on personal values, background and understanding. Like other habits, frames can be changed; this, though, takes effort and commitment. Big picture thinking is an example of challenging a frame of reference.

The process of mentally stepping back, up or away from a frame is called 'reframing'. Shifting perspective in this way is healthy, creative and leads to innovative ideas. This refers to making a conscious choice to interpret the world in a new way. The first step is to identify the frame given to a situation. This usually consists of the story or interpretation which individuals give to events they observe.

The facts of an exchange are often indisputable, but the frames given to the exchange are often as different as the number of people who observe it. For example, every Friday, three colleagues meet at the coffee machine and talk about their weekend plans. The boss observes this and frames the exchange as: these three are always wasting time. The office 'outcast' frames the observed meeting as: those three are always together and are such close friends. The office 'organiser' frames them as: an opportunity to embarrass all three together into contributing to the United Charities Fund.

Based on their different priorities and frames of reference, each person interprets what they see and hear in a manner unique to them. The point is for leaders to recognise this about themselves and accept that theirs is just one of many possible interpretations. Those who are unwilling to see this limit themselves and their leadership ability.

Although they can be praised for single-mindedness, this is a short step away from rigid thinking. Their challenge is to slow down the process of interpreting events until all of the facts are known and then to question whether there are any reframes possible for what is seen and heard.

Activity
- Choose a new magazine or journal. Look through this until a picture attracts your attention
- Without reading any explanation for the picture, interpret what you see
- This is your frame
- Now, look at the picture again. Challenge yourself to tell a completely different story about the events and people in this picture
- Imagine:
  - different emotions being expressed
  - different motives and intentions
  - different power relationships
- This is your reframe

The skill of reframing is a valuable one for leaders. It encourages development of insight as well as mental flexibility. It also has direct application for creation of vision. When individuals are locked into interpreting what they see and hear as a single frame, they lack the capacity to envision. The distant light on the hill for them is always going to be just another all-night petrol station. Reframing creates the possibility of new outcomes and new ideas. Leaders need the zest which a truly open mind allows them to experience.

Checklist

- Think of an event during the day which was important to you
- How did you interpret what occurred?
- Is this the usual way for you to interpret events?
- If so, can you summarise your mental habits when this kind of event occurs?
- Did you make an effort to discover other possible interpretations of what occurred?
- If not, reframe the event now
- Consider one, if there is at least one, positive outcome as a result of reframing this event
- What is the big picture for this event?

Taking charge

The seventh step to successful leadership draws upon the skills, knowledge and experience gained through this week-long programme. Each step of the process focused on a leadership essential. These include personal development and awareness, how to relate to colleagues and understanding motivation, the right use of power, communication skills, decision-making and the development of vision.

Improved performance means that leaders need to take charge of their thinking about each of these topics as well as take charge of changing their behaviour. Today's activities emphasise a review of the week. This involves assessing the strengths and weaknesses of leadership performance in terms of the six topics included in this programme. The task is to identify what went well and what went badly. This provides information to create a plan of action for further leadership development.

Sunday review: developing awareness

Leaders need to know their strengths and limitations. This is the basis for their learning how to stretch their ability with new skills, knowledge and experience.

- Consider your overall performance as a leader during the week
- It helps to remember how you began work each day
- What qualities did you express consistently throughout the week?
- What attention did you give to creating positive relationships with your colleagues?
- List three strengths in the way you made contact with your colleagues
- How can you build upon these strengths?
- List three weaknesses in your behaviour towards your colleagues
- What quality or qualities do you need to develop in order to improve upon these weaknesses?

Monday review: understanding people

Successful leaders know how to speak directly to people's needs, hopes and dreams. Recognising and respecting these creates bonds of loyalty and trust between leaders and their supporters. It is also important to recognise what motivates people and that different people feel rewarded in varying ways.

- Consider how able you were to identify with your colleagues during the week
- It helps to focus on their reactions to you when you asked them to do something for you
- Do any of your colleagues merge together as part of an indistinct group?
- How can you learn more about each person so that their individual strengths and weaknesses become clear?
- List three strengths for the way you go about understanding other people
- How can you build upon these strengths?
- List three weaknesses for the way you go about understanding other people
- What pattern of behaviour do you need to change in order to improve upon these weaknesses?

Tuesday review: power and authority

Leaders have power, authority and responsibility. They need to exercise these and also empower their colleagues to take initiative and responsibility as well. It requires confidence for leaders to invite challenge, questions and comments from their colleagues. It is also a sign of strong leadership.

- Consider the way in which you exercised power during the week
- It helps to remember those activities for which you have responsibility

- Were you able to distinguish the kind of power best suited to each situation?
- List three strengths about the way you exercised power or took responsibility
- How can you build upon these strengths?
- List three weaknesses in your style of leadership
- What do you need to do in order to feel safe about trying a different style?

Wednesday review: communication

Communication skills benefit all areas of life, not just leadership development. Although they are often taken for granted, these skills are highly complex. Even casual information exchange creates the potential for complete misunderstanding.

- Consider your overall communication performance during the week
- It helps to focus on exchanges with people you know less well. These rely more on your having skills for successful information exchange
- What areas of social skill need further attention and what steps can you take to develop these social skills?
- List three strengths for your ability to listen and three strengths for your ability to present information through speaking
- How can you build upon all of these strengths?

- List three weaknesses for your listening skills and three weaknesses for your ability to present information through speaking
- How can you transform these and improve your performance?

Thursday review: decision-making

Decisiveness is an essential quality for leadership and decision-making skills are required for effective performance. It takes discrimination and judgement to prioritise information and set goals in preparation for making decisions.

- Consider your decision-making activity during the week
- It helps to focus on a decision which caused you some stress
- Did you use a systematic approach, that is, consider information in a rational way or consider priorities and set clear goals?
- Did any decision 'just get made' because circumstances took over and made the decision for you?
- List three strengths in the way that you make decisions
- How can you build upon these strengths?
- List three weaknesses in the way that you make decisions
- What actions can you take to improve upon these weaknesses?

Friday review: creating a vision

This development area is most difficult to master and yet yields the greatest reward. The ability to imagine new possibilities and create new solutions is highly valued. It is suggested that with determined practice, anyone can learn to work creatively with vision.

- Consider your performance as a manager or administrator during the week
- How frequently did you invite new ideas or comments from your colleagues by asking them 'why not?'
- Did you focus all of your management time on solving current problems and dealing with routine business?
- How can you give yourself more time to create vision in both your personal and professional life?
- How can you actively work to achieve more of your potential?
- List three strengths for the way you are able to see the larger context for a single activity
- How can you build upon these?
- List three weaknesses for the way in which you review new solutions and ideas
- How can you challenge yourself to be more creative?

Bennis, Warren, *On Becoming a Leader*, Wokingham, England: Addison-Wesley, 1994.

Collus, Jim, *Good to Great*. HarperCollins, 2001

Ferrucci, Piero, *What We May Be*, London: Aquarian Press, 1990.

Larkin, T.J. and Larkin, Sandar, *Communication change: winning employee support for new business goals*. McGraw-Hill, 2000.

Maslow, Abraham, *Motivation and Personality*, New York: Harper & Row, 1954.

O'Connor, Carol A., *The Handbook for Organisational Change*, Maidenhead, England: McGraw-Hill, 1993.

O'Connor, Carol, A. Visit her website at www.visiprac.com or email her direct at info@visiprac.com.

For information

on other

IN A **WEEK** titles

go to

www.inaweek.co.uk